George Wythe Munford

The jewels of Virginia

A lecture, delivered by invitation of the Hollywood Memorial Association

in Richmond

George Wythe Munford

The jewels of Virginia
A lecture, delivered by invitation of the Hollywood Memorial Association in Richmond

ISBN/EAN: 9783337135164

Printed in Europe, USA, Canada, Australia, Japan

Cover: Foto ©Andreas Hilbeck / pixelio.de

More available books at **www.hansebooks.com**

The Jewels of Virginia:

A LECTURE,

DELIVERED BY INVITATION OF THE

HOLLYWOOD MEMORIAL ASSOCIATION

IN RICHMOND, JANUARY 18, 1867,

BY

Col. GEORGE WYTHE MUNFORD,

Of Gloucester, Va.

[Published for the benefit of the Association.]

RICHMOND:
GARY & CLEMMITT, PRINTERS.
1867.

F

LECTURE.

One of the most difficult things to accomplish is the composition of good toasts. To make them worthy of note they should be sententious, full of meaning, and like the champaigne in which they ought to be drunk, spirited and buoyant. Of the great number I have heard, the only one I will recall was delivered many years ago by the great Carolinian. It was "Virginia! Like the mother of the Gracchi, when asked for her jewels, she points to her sons." This sentiment, rich with classic beauty, high compliment and sparkling brilliancy, I have adopted as the theme of my discourse on the present occasion.

But I have so seldom addressed a public audience, and especially of late, that I feel like the aged minstrel:

> "Amid the strings his fingers stray'd,
> And an uncertain warbling made,
> And oft he shook his hoary head."

If I shall gain his reassured confidence, I may begin to "talk anon

> Of good earl Francis, dead and gone;
> And of earl Walter, rest him God!
> A braver ne'er to battle rode."

I may make an effort to bring to remembrance the great, the good, the wise and the brave of Virginia, who were characterized by the great and good, the wise and brave Calhoun as the "jewels" she wears, and to which she points with exalted pride as ornaments that have made her famous in story, and given her glory and immortality. There has been no son of hers of any repute in her councils, or the councils of the nation, for the last fifty years, that I have not seen and known. I have had opportunity to scan their public actions and writings, their persons and lineaments, the character of their minds, the intonation of their voice, their style of oratory, their modes of thought, the principles they inculcate, the parties upon whose altars they poured their incense, the aims and objects they had in view.

But where shall I begin? Which casket shall I open? Her house is full of them—jaspers, sapphires, chalcedonies and emeralds. In the quaint language of St. John the evangelist, at the close of his gospel, I may say, and there are also many things which the great men of Virginia have accomplished, "the which, if they should be written, every one, I suppose that even the world itself could not contain the books that should be written." I shall have then to pick and to choose, and while I would do injustice to none, by omission, I must per force leave some of them on the pedestals, upon whose superstructure some Houdon, or Crawford, or Rogers, may rear their form sublime. And then again there are thousands who have never entered her councils, whose charity and hospitality, and rare intellects and virtues, have made Virginia lovely and of good report, and spread her renown from pole to pole.

Besides the oaks of her forests, there are roses and lillies in her vales, and

> "Though large the forest monarch throws
> His leafy shade,
> Yet sweet the juicy hawthorne grows
> Adown the glade."

Of all her brilliants, none can compare with her Washington, the greatest of all the Kohinoors of ancient or of modern times. Every chisel and every brush has essayed to develop his character and actions; every pen endeavored

to describe and beautify both; every flower and leaf have
been woven and twined around him; every heart has
poured forth its love; every tongue uttered his name with
loud acclaim, and all the nations praise him. I name the
name of Washington, simply because my subject is Virginia's jewels, and I could not omit her purest, most pellu-
cid, unblemished diamond.

In the mysterious book of Revelation we read of one
"that was, and is not, and yet is;" and this language
seems to convey a contradiction in terms. But when I
contemplate the life of Washington, I can understand how
it may be true; for he was, and is not, and yet is. He
lived, he is dead, and yet he lives. We may well imagine
that his living soul has found a blissful paradise. We may
well imagine that one of the four and twenty seats which
are round and about the throne of Jehovah has been reserved for him, and that he occupies the place of one of
the four and twenty elders that were clothed in white raiment with crowns of gold upon their heads.

But, more than this, he lives on earth, he endures in his
precepts, in his writings, in his prophetic warnings, in his
matchless example, in the institution of learning which he
endowed, and to which the fame of the second Washington, now at its head, has given a new attractive force; by
which the minds that will be enlightened there will en-
lighten others, and so on, wave upon wave extending and
enlarging through endless ages. And besides, we have a
living witness in the person of Governor Wise, (another of
Virginia's jewels), who happily reminds us, in glowing
language, that George Washington lives in another sense;
for "in Houdon's marble we have the form and feature,
the limb and lineament, the configuration and proportion,
the stature and posture, and we have enlivening all, illu-
mining all, the mien, and manner, and majesty of the man,
the breath as well as the body, the grandeur of the moral
greatness of the very soul of the living Washington!"

But how long he may be permitted to live in the capitol

in peace I know not. The deeds that are being done in these days ought to make his bones restless in their tomb; for if aliens to our soil can mutilate and deface the college he endowed, demolish its apparatus and destroy its libraries; if they could lay in ashes the beautiful and imposing buildings of the Virginia Military Institute, and rob it of all that could be appropriated as trophies, and displace from its pedestal that statue in bronze which Virginia had erected there, as another "endearing proof of her gratitude to her living son," what may they not do? How long his bones may be permitted to rest in Virginia soil I know not; for if they can obliterate at one blow our ancient boundaries, and erect a new state by the consent of the sham representatives of three or four counties, and at their pleasure take from us county after county, and annex them to another state, why may they not give Mount Vernon to Massachusetts, and give her the title to claim our consecrated relic as her own, her living son? Yes, they may take that "West Augusta," upon which he relied as his refuge and safeguard, and give it to another; they may take from his mother Virginia her rights and her heritage; they make take his monuments and grind them to powder, and sow it on the fields, but the father will live in the hearts of his children, and he will live forever "to the world an immortal example of true glory."

If he is dead, let his disinterestedness live. Let his letter to the general assembly live, in which they were told "that when first called to the command of the American forces, he resolved, and since then he had invariably adhered to the resolution, to shut his hands against every pecuniary recompense." Let "the endowments of the hero and the virtues of the patriot" live. Let his endeavors to establish the liberties of his country live, whether those liberties under the pressure of modern radicalism survive or perish. Let the great works for the improvement of his native state, and which were encouraged by his patronage, live. Let the great avenue of the state which he designated be opened up, until at every pulsation her life-blood as it gushes from her heart shall flow from one extremity to the other. Above all, if we are ever restored to the Union, and awarded our equal station by the side of the other states, then let the spirit of amity and of mutual deference and concession which he invoked as indispensably necessary at the adoption of the constitution be revived, and let the era of harmony and peace bring forth its living fruit, to be enjoyed equally by all, now and forever.

And if it would be improper to omit the name of Washington, for the same reason I must mention the grand old orator Patrick Henry, whose eloquence sparkles, even at second hand, like coruscations from the tips of brilliants; and the great and revered George Mason, the author of the Bill of Rights and of the first Constitution for Virginia, the composition of which required the learning of the scholar, the wisdom of the statesman and the purity of the patriot. Every one who has dipped into the history of the colonies knows that Henry was the foremost to draw the sword in defence of the rights of the country, and was the originator of the three greatest test measures of that epoch, the resolutions against the Stamp Act, the resolutions for placing the colony in military array, and equipping her armies for the field, and the resolutions instructing our delegates in congress to declare the colonies free and independent. They well know that he was the animating spirit of the revolution, leading and swaying public opinion, and boldly guiding it for the public good. None but intrepid men, in such times, can induce the masses to attempt an overthrow of established governments. Men who are calculating chances of success, and looking to self-promotion or self-interest, are looked upon with cold indifference. When the masses of a community are chafing under wrong and oppression, each one of them feels that singly he is powerless, and therefore for a long time they smother their discontent, and mutter hatred between their teeth;

but when at length an upright, disinterested, bold patriot arises, with burning oratory on his lips, and a proud consciousness of rectitude stamped upon his brow, and animates the crowd, and gives them hope of success, he becomes their mouthpiece, gives utterance to their stifled feelings, and is able to move and hurl the masses whithersoever he will. This was Patrick Henry; thus he threw his soul into the cause, and waked the living spirit of rebellion, hurling it against the old government, and causing its overthrow and annihilation.

So, on the other hand, when men have been roused and agitated, and induced with all their energies to upturn and destroy their government and laws, and anarchy begins to reign, the wealthy and the prudent begin to take alarm, and eagerly look around for some balance wheel to regulate and control the disordered mass, and bring system and order out of chaos. Then some man equally bold, equally wise, and equally patriotic and disinterested, is required to compose the popular mind by giving form and life to the desire to protect property, and life and honor. A declaration of rights is necessary, a form of government is essential, with all its departments complete, to give stability, and to ensure calm and repose. And this was the duty which was assigned to George Mason, and which he accomplished with unsurpassed ability. For this he drew the Virginia Bill of Rights, which announces the very essence of the great principles and doctrines of freedom from the earliest times, the elemental ideas, which constitute the foundations upon which society rests, and upon which all good and free governments are constituted. These principles afforded the pabulum for thought, and were the short pithy axioms which men could easily understand, and for which they were ready to risk their lives and their fortunes, and for the maintenance of which they intended to peril everything within their power. And then when they had grasped the principles, there came forth from his brain the form of government, which embodied these principles, and afforded evidence of the stability which was so much needed, and which had the effect to compose the prudent, to restrain the vicious, and protect all in the acquirement of property and in the maintenance of right.

Thus we had the orator to rouse, animate, lead, upturn and destroy the old government, and the statesman to compose, calm, regulate and govern. And then to show the confidence reposed in the orator and destructionist, the general assembly elected Henry the first governor, to establish and make solid the new government, to put it in motion, to see that all its machinery worked smoothly, without jostle or derangement, and to protect and defend all interests entrusted to his governmental care.

Such gems as these I cannot omit, though I have been constrained to limit myself almost entirely to the contemplation of the jewels that I have personally seen, or with whom I have had personal intercourse.

Nor can I omit, next to these great men, among the architects of Virginia's fame, her sons, Jefferson, Madison and Monroe. Every one, without hesitation, would designate them as jewels worthy to ornament the brow of any state, but at the same time it would be universally admitted that it would be next to impossible to present any characteristic of their lives, which histories and biographies have not already given. I cannot pass them by unnoticed, and yet I do not expect to add one jot or tittle to their exalted fame. Each one was himself a monument of industry, of intelligence, of consistent and devoted purpose, of patriotism pure and fearless, and of rare and far-reaching philanthropy. They all ascended the ladder of fame successively, and each as he advanced paused at each round, to make an enduring mark for the benefit of posterity, and for the glory of his country. Few of those present, I imagine, have ever seen these great men, or listened to their pleasant and instructive words. I have had the good fortune to see and converse with each of them, and have a most pleasing recollection of their per-

2

sonal appearance and delightful manners. There are portraits and monuments of each, to which reference may be had. In the hall of the house of delegates there is a full length portrait of Mr. Jefferson, taken by Catlin, which was purchased by a few gentlemen of this city, and placed there as a memento of his person, and a memorial of their devotion to his character. You have all seen, too, the colossal statue in bronze by Crawford on the Washington monument. Besides these, the general assembly authorized Alexander Galt, of Norfolk, a young Virginia sculptor of great promise, to execute a marble statue, which has been placed at the University.

As I remember the great patriot and sage, he was tall, slender, and remarkably erect, with a small head and thin hair, originally reddish, but so intermingled with grey as to have softened it to a pleasant hue, with mild, speaking blue eyes, emitting the rays of his brightened intellect, and a countenance composed, yet frank and enlightened.

Of Mr. Madison there are doubtless many likenesses, but the chief are those taken by Stuart in 1803, by Catlin in 1831, and by Longacre in 1833, three years before his death. His person as he appeared to me when in the Convention of 1829–'30, was that of a Virginia gentleman of the olden school, of medium stature, dressed in a plain suit of black cloth, with short knee breeches clasped at the knees with silver buckles, black silk stockings, and shoes fastened with silver buckles too, with powdered hair, full over the ears, and smoothly brushed and tied behind. Add to these a speaking eye, a fine forehead, a benevolent countenance, a cheerful, healthy complexion, tinged with the ruby of a moderate quantity of the best old madeira, with a hand open, and a purse ready to minister to the wants of the destitute and poor, and a mind enlightened by copious drafts from the pierian spring, and you will have a good idea of Mr. Madison as I remember him.

Mr. Monroe was taller than Mr. Madison, but the former, at the same period, had become very feeble and much broken, his face exceedingly wrinkled, and complexion pale and sallow. In the last year of his presidency, when I saw him in the white-house transacting business with his secretary of state John Quincy Adams, I would have described him as another specimen of the Virginia gentleman, affable and courteous, whose soul had abandoned recreation and pleasure, and devoted itself to the cares, and toils, and troubles of great affairs, and whose constant thoughts were the welfare and honor of a great people.

Mr. Jefferson and Mr. Monroe were educated at William and. Mary college, the alma mater of as many great men as ever adorned the halls of any literary institution, and their free and unrestrained intercourse with the polished society of old Williamsburg gave them an ease and elegance of manners, which, in after life, was mellowed and chastened by the refinement of the most elegant circles of America and of foreign courts. Mr. Madison was educated at Princeton college, and he, too, possessed a fascination and grace, a simplicity and frankness that repelled formality, and lent a charm to his society that was exceedingly delightful. If at any period of their history the people had occasion for men of pure and irreproachable lives, of enlightened intellect, with judgment and prudence, armed with argument and reason, with a quiver full of the choicest arrows from all the armories of literature, of unruffled temper, of firm and decided action, simple in dress, easy of access, frank and artless in conversation, yet enlivening and instructive, they would turn with undoubting faith to these men as representatives fit for any office.

They accordingly successively occupied all of the political offices fit for such a rare combination of qualifications, and every office was honored by their presence. Each of them has left among the archives of his office enduring evidences of industry and extraordinary powers. Mr. Jefferson and Mr. Monroe were members of the general assembly, members of conventions, members of congress, governors, ministers to foreign courts, secretary of state.

Mr. Jefferson was vice president, and both were presidents of the United States. Mr. Madison occupied all of the same offices, except that he never held a diplomatic appointment, nor was governor of the state. Mr. Jefferson and Mr. Madison were each visitors and rectors of the University, and Mr. Madison and Mr. Monroe were each in the convention to revise the constitution of Virginia in 1829–'30. Each served as president of the United States for eight years; but Mr. Monroe was the only one of all the presidents who came into office with every electoral vote save one.

I had the pleasure on several occasions of hearing Mr. Jefferson in the unreserve of private conversation. Such men necessarily enchain the attention of others, and their reminiscences of events and incidents in their previous lives, and in their deep research after knowledge, are exceedingly entertaining. On one occasion, with an enchanting pleasantry, he was giving a description of the offices and character of the muses and graces, and of the poesy of the ancient mythology, and being myself a young man then, I was particularly struck with his remark, "that he had been amused in his reading to find that upon antique gems Vulcan, the artizan of Olympus, was represented in his workshop forging arrows for the little god Cupid." Our fair daughters and bachelor sons will have to keep a sharp look out, for if in these days the deformed old god, with his accumulated experience and skill, should be still engaged in his ancient occupation, it will be exceedingly difficult to shun those arrows, feathered and keenly tipped by a master workman, and sped with unerring certainty by a very cunning and wary little bowman. Mr. Jefferson, on the occasion referred to, glided into the theme of the monuments of antiquity, and dwelt upon the perfection of ancient architecture, and the magnificence of ancient temples and public buildings, and said that he had selected for the model of the capitol at Richmond the Maison Carre, or temple of Nismes, which though of more modern date was remarkable for its beauty and architectural proportions. That model is still preserved in the capitol; but any one who will examine it, will discern in the building which was erected many departures from the design, particularly in the change of the attic into a basement, and in the construction of the columns to the portico, which are of the same diameter from the base to the capitol, and in the omission of the steps to the portico, which add grace and usefulness in the model.

Mr. Jefferson's mind at that time was engrossed with the erection of the University, and his conversation continually ran upon that topic. It was the pet of his old age, and he petted it, because he hoped at no distant day that all the orders of architecture would be developed there. And he expressed the fond desire to build up the institution, for the purpose of preparing Virginia's sons to become the instructors of future generations, and to diffuse her principles and policy among the other states, instead of having the minds of our own youth polluted and corrupted by imported teachers, who had overrun the state and taken possession of our academies and primary schools. He had the sagacity to discern the necessity and the importance of institutions at which the highest branches are taught, to ensure for all time the capacity to teach all the sciences and arts, and thus give to Virginia the power and glory that enlightened intellect will ever command.

Nothing that his great mind touched upon was without its interest. He had been the great reformer of the age— had warred against long established abuses, and against every principle that tended to perpetuate the old aristocracy, or to strengthen the hand of power. He had laid his axe at the very root of the tree, and eradicated the laws of primogeniture, of entails, and of a governmental religion; and though these subjects were intimately interwoven with our whole system, and constituted its fibres, and nerves, and muscles, yet he possessed the popularity and power to destroy them, and to erect a new system upon their ruins. He was the founder of the republican party of that day, and the master builder of the democracy, and he pursued the old federal party with the bosom of destruction, and for this reason was subjected to as much hostility and vituperation as ever fell to the lot of any man, but he pursued his purpose with undiverted aim.

The three great acts of his life which he deemed worthy to constitute the inscription on his monument were the declaration of independence, the act for establishing religious freedom, and the establishment of the University of Virginia. Not his writings, which were upon almost every conceivable subject, and which displayed unusual erudition, deep research, universality of taste and unsurpassed industry and accuracy; not his correspondence with all the publicists and scholars of the age, marked as it was by originality of thought and fearlessness of expression, and stored with the consecrated lore of the classics, and with fruit from all the granaries of the earth. Not his acquisition of Louisiana, the master stroke of his policy while president, which unlocked the Mississippi and its tributaries, and brought into existence the millions of human beings, who have since teemed like magic in the vast country through which these inland seas flow, with myriads of productions that have sprung from their industry, enterprise and capital, displaying a wealth and magnificence that have made the power and. might of this nation the astonishment of all people; not his political acts with his party victories and triumphs; not the offices he filled, with the great men around him, agitating and composing great questions and guiding a nation's destinies; but, the emanations of his mind—independence, religous freedom and education.

I have sometimes thought, if Mr. Jefferson could come back into the world with the indignant feelings that inspired him when he penned the declaration of independence, and could take in at a glance the enormities that have been perpetrated upon the southern people since his departure from the earth; could see his beloved Virginia, whose voice was once so potential in the national councils, now palsied by the infliction of wrongs more aggravated than those perpetrated upon the colonies by the British king; could see her with diminished territory, taxed without representation, not permitted in any department of the government to raise a finger of warning or utter a word of reprobation against those who are warring against constitutions and reeking their vengeance upon her people; could see her citizens deprived of property without their consent, governed by laws intended to oppress them, not assented to by their representatives; her state laws suspended by subordinate military commanders by the mere exercise of their orders; trial by jury abolished and substituted by mock trials held by petty military officers having no knowledge of law, and not recognizing the binding obligation of constitutions; the liberty of the press assailed by the arrest of editors and the seizure of their presses and papers; standing armies quartered upon her in time of peace, and every aggravation of misrule impending or threatened.—If he could see all this perpetrated by authority of the federal government, not in time of war, but after the restoration of peace has been proclaimed, and after all the states have returned to their allegiance and become loyal to the government, he would blot from his monument that he was the author of the declaration, and mourn that in so short a time all its principles had been subverted and destroyed. If he did not do this, he would attempt to exercise the once acknowledged right of petition, and send to congress a remonstrance, burning with brands plucked from the altar of liberty, breathing the inspired sentiments of a free soul, filled with the exalted pride of a freeman, who felt that freedom was his inheritance, and that a virtuous nation could not deprive a son descending from noble ancestors who secured the liberty of that nation of his just privileges and inestimable birthright.

If he were on earth he would at least rejoice that the other highest creation of his brain, religious liberty, had as

yet stood the wreck of nearly every other hope, and that
the pet of his old age, the University, still survives.   Of
these, he would have cause still to be proud, and every man
in the state has cause to be thankful.   It is some consolation at least to reflect that we have one right not yet de-
nied,—"That Almighty God hath created the mind free;
that all attempts to influence it by temporal punishment or
burdens, or by civil incapacitations, tend only to beget hy-
pocrisy and meanness."   (It would be well if our rulers
would weigh these words in their application to other
rights!) "That all men shall be free to profess, and by argument to maintain, their opinions in matters of religion."
Every temple that rears its beautiful spire to the clouds and
adorns our cities, and every lowly church in a sequestered
grove, is a monument to the sacredness of these principles
and to the assertion that "truth is great and will prevail;
that she is the proper and sufficient antagonist of error and
has nothing to fear from the conflict, unless by human in-
terposition disarmed of her natural weapons, free argument
and debate—errors ceasing to be dangerous when it is permitted freely to contradict them."   We have one other
consolation too, that the University and our other noble
educational institutions and charities have been permitted to
exist, and that the higher institutions will in time send down
bright minds to elevate the lower and bring them in turn
to the higher, to be improved in a more expanded degree,
establishing a current of learning through all the ramifica-
tions of society; like wisdom descending from the mind
of the Almighty, permeating all the minds upon earth in
different degrees, but preparing all as they improve and
are exalted, to be adapted to inhabit the regions of eternal
bliss.

If, my friends, any of you desire to know something
more of Mr. Madison—if you desire to glance at his writings
and his speeches, and the colouring and shading which
made his bright and eventful life glorious, I must refer
you to William C. Rives, the gifted biographer, another

of Virginia's jewels. You will find him devoting his retirement to develop the genius and virtues of the patriot
sage, and endeavoring to transmit to posterity a biography
worthy of his noble theme. But if you are not content,
and still desire some specimen of his power of argument,
and his manner of forging a chain of reasoning, I can only
invite you to read his report and resolutions of '98 and
'99. A finer specimen of a lucid style and a more overwhelming and convincing argument can scarcely be found
in the English language. They produced the desired effect
in their day, and the alien and sedition laws against which
they were leveled, which were proved to be utterly un-
constitutional, were suffered to expire by their own limitation, and were never subsequently revived. They ought
to have a similar effect now, in restraining latitudinarian
constructions of the constitution. But men have no occasion for forced or strained constructions now: when congress, or its leading men, in their mad career rush up
against the constitution, they do not hesitate a moment,
but crack their whips and drive right onward through constitutions and laws, and over principles and rights. If you
are not satisfied still, and wish to have an inkling of his
prophetic vision, listen while I give you a short extract, de-
tailing his apprehensions of the encroachments of the legislative department of the government. It saddens the heart
when we look around us and see how the prophesies of
these men are being fulfilled—how the encroachments of
power are sweeping away all constitutional restraints. In
former days we were accustomed to look with anxiety on
the usurpations of the executive department, and to hurl
our thunders at the one man power. Now, we are looking
with terror at the great malstrom of legislative misrule,
which is drawing into its maddening and muddy whirl-
pool all the powers of the government, and usurping powers never contemplated by the wildest Utopean. He says:
"Experience assures us that the efficacy of providing written constitutions has been greatly overrated, and that

3

some more adequate defence is indispensably necessary for the more feeble against the more powerful members of the government. The legislative department is everywhere extending the sphere of its activity, and drawing all power into its impetuous vortex." "The founders of the republic seem never to have recollected the danger from legislative usurpations, which by assembling all power in the same hands must lead to the same tyranny as is threatened by executive usurpations. But in a representative republic, where the executive magistrate is carefully limited, both in the extent and duration of its power, and where the legislative power is exercised by an assembly, which is inspired by a supposed influence over the people, with an intrepid confidence in its own strength, which is sufficiently numerous to feel all the passions which actuate a multitude, yet not so numerous as to be incapable of pursuing the objects of its passions, by means which reason prescribes, *it is against the enterprising ambition of this department that the people ought to indulge all their jealousy and exhaust all their precautions.*"

And I cannot resist the inclination to quote a passage from Mr. Jefferson's pen, of similar import. In his impressive language, he says: "All the powers of government, legislative, executive and judiciary, result to the legislative body. The concentrating these in the same hands is precisely the definition of despotic government. It will be no alleviation that those powers will be exercised by a plurality of hands, and not by a single one. One hundred and seventy-three despots would surely be as oppressive as one."

Were these men speaking of the present congress? Were they warning us against the enterprising ambition of the legislative department of these times? If the present congress succeed in concentrating all the power they are now striving to obtain in their own hands, then we shall have precisely the definition of despotic government verified and intensified. Virginia, dismembered, disheart-

ened, spirit-broken Virginia, cannot interpose as she once
did, for she is helpless and almost hopeless; but there are
other states—not in the southern clime, but in the frozen
zone—who may, like Mary, the mother of the Saviour,
"keep all these things and ponder them in their hearts."
We are powerless to restrain, can do nothing but fold the
arms and shake the head. But other states will come in
for their share in time. The lion hunts his prey day by
day, and when he has slaked his thirst with the blood of
one victim, seeks another. Wisdom looks afar off, and by
the signs which she has noted, marks the coming tempest,
and prepares her refuge before it sweeps the ocean and the
land.

But I hurry on. If I touch on the character, or actions,
or writings of any of these men, the materials grow, en-
large, expand. I have no time to dwell even for a moment
upon any of the interesting incidents of the war with England which occurred during Mr. Madison's administration.
If I were disposed to eulogize the old flag, and to paint
daring deeds, brilliant achievements and thrilling events, I
might pause for a second, for we had a right to claim a full
share of the honors and the glory of those days, as well as
of the days of the revolution. We could run up "Union
jack" then. We could glory in the motto, "Don't give
up the ship" then. Our men were there, our guns pealed
forth their thunders, our ships sent the ships of old England to Davy Jones' locker, their glories were wreathed
around us. Our money in full share was devoted to the
service, for the spirit of the south was "millions for defence, not a cent for tribute," and the blood of our sons
was freely spilled. It was our home, and our country we
defended, and we had a right to share all the fame. Then
our rights were respected, our honor was revered. Virginia was at the helm, and the constitution was the compass. The stars and stripes were the emblem of an Union,
whose honor and faith were untarnished and spotless.
State rights were venerated. A gallant ship bore the

name of the Constitution, and the gallant tars who were aboard of her fought with desperation, because she was the type of the fundamental law. She was nicknamed Old Ironsides, to indicate that neither shot nor bomb could pierce her impregnable sides. Such was the love they bore her, that even when she was unfit for service, they refused to permit her to be broken up, and every one exclaimed with the poet:

> O, better that her shattered hulk
> Should sink beneath the wave;
> Her thunders shook the mighty deep,
> And there should be her grave."

And, alas! if the government had continued to respect the instrument as they did the emblem; if they had not warred against the one while they adored the other, our own Confederate government never would have lived its short, glorious and honored life. But while the latter existed, it performed one illustrious act at least, that will ring in future time, and glitter in story and in song. As the congress was the chief violator of the constitution, and a ship had been christened the Congress in honor of it, and was its emblem, the iron-clad Virginia of the Confederate States conquered the emblem and sent its flames to the skies and its ashes to the mighty deep. And at the same time sunk the Cumberland, and riddled the Minesota, and scared off the Roanoke, and peppered the St. Lawrence, and disabled two gunboats, drove off the Erricson and silenced the forts. That was glory enough for one day.

If the constitution should ever be respected again; if the olden times should ever return; if men, like the patriots of a better age, should once more raise their hands and their voices to protect, not only the rights of minorities but State rights as they were, once acknowledged, and the rights of the humblest and poorest citizen, and we could say, "Inasmuch as ye did it to the least of these ye

did it unto me." Then we might be able once more to
say:

"By the death of the brave! by the God in the skies,
There's life in the old land yet."

Then the wise and the good might have a brighter hope for
a better day.

In the Convention of 1829–'30, the greatest assembly of
Virginia jewels that was ever exhibited to an admiring
country, I had an opportunity to witness a little incident,
which I mention simply to show how great men will sometimes be appalled. Mr. Monroe, the old soldier of the
revolution, the friend of Washington, Jefferson and Madison, and beloved by every body, had been unanimously
elected president of the convention. The men of other
days with their mellowed fame, and the men who were preparing to take their places with the fresh garlands they
were daily gathering, were assembled around him. They
were in the hall of the house of delegates, seated in the
old benches which time had consecrated; the president in
the old walnut chair, a curious specimen of antiquity,
which, even in my day, I have seen with the coat of arms
of Great Britian emblazoned on its frontlet; the room
filled to its utmost capacity, when Mr. Madison rose and
addressed the chair. The reporters seized their pens.
The convention rose in a body. Every man stood. The
great man assayed his voice, and finding it too weak to fill
the compass of the hall, advanced from his seat quite to
the secretary's table. Nearly the entire convention rushed
around him. He was confused by the unusual circum-
stance, faltered once or twice, but then proceeded, and
while his language was chaste and pure, his ideas did not
flow in a connected chain, the point and the strength was
wanting, which he possessed when "he was wont to pull the
arrow to its head on the strongest bow and let it fly with
all its power." Few of those who surrounded him could

hear his remarks, and none of the spectators could catch a syllable.

In the evening, as secretary, I went as usual to Mr. Monroe's apartment to read to him the day's proceedings, as required by the rules. Mr. Madison came in. It was delightful to witness the cordiality of the old cronies, and the boyish playfulness with which the one accosted the other. It reminded me of the song

> "John Anderson, my Joe, John,
>   We've clomed the hill thegither,
> And mony a canty day, John,
>   We've had we ane anither:
> Now we maun totter down, John,
>   In hand and hand we'll go,
> And sleep together at the foot,
>   John Anderson, my Joe."

In a few moments the reporter of the debates entered and asked Mr. Madison to run over the notes he had sketched of his remarks. "Sir," said he, "I would not have you publish that speech as it was delivered for any consideration. Did you not perceive that I had the buck ague? The situation in which I was placed, the knowledge that much was expected of me, the feebleness of my voice, the rush of the convention around me, unnerved and sealed my brain and it would not work. I will give you the remarks I intended to make, but not that speech."

It is remarkable to see how many of the principles announced by all of these remarkable men live to keep up their fame. We see their effects every day,—they are producing results in the world now that can scarcely be appreciated. As an evidence of this, I will barely mention the Monroe doctrine, which announced to the world that the United States would not permit the nations of the old hemisphere to interfere with the concerns of the new. Now, we see the time has already come when this principle is guiding the government, and the Napoleons of modern times have been warned that they have stepped beyond the boundary prescribed, and they must unclutch their grasp from Mexico and withdraw their troops. But I am compelled to close this casket of jewels and hasten to another.

Mr. Madison died on the 28th of June, 1836. Had he lived a few days longer he would have expired on the 4th of July, the day which, memorable as it is, was made still more memorable by the death of Jefferson, Adams and Monroe. He is buried at Montpelier, in the county of Orange, and the words James Madison, and the date of his birth and death, constitute the only inscription on his tomb.

There is in the cemetery at Hollywood, on the beautiful hill which overlooks the river, a monument erected by the state in honor of Mr. Monroe. On one side are the words, "James Monroe. Born in Westmoreland county 28th April, 1758. Died in the city of New York 4th July, 1831. By order of the general assembly his remains were removed to this cemetery 5th July, 1858, as an evidence of the affection of Virginia for her good and honest son." On the other side: "The eminent services performed by this patriot for his country are enduring monuments of his wisdom and virtue."

After having glanced at these antique gems, we come to look at more modern jewels, which we cherish not only for their intrinsic value, but for the associations which surround them. I come to bestow a kind remembrance upon John Tyler, another of Virginia's sons, whom she prized for the services he rendered, and the noble qualities of his head and heart. When I was first elected clerk of the house of delegates, his voice was among the first that I heard ringing in its hall, and his hand the first that gave me a welcome to the position I occupied. And there was a charm about the voice that won upon the heart, and a warmth in the grip of the hand that felt cordial, and an attraction in the countenance and manner of the man that drew you to him with irresistible power. When he was

elected governor, which was at the same session of the
general assembly, I was welcomed in the same way in the
governor's mansion and in the executive chamber, and such
was his ease and familiarity, that everybody could approach
him without the least restraint, and he transacted business
with such promptness and kindness, that it was a pleasure
to have official intercourse with him. He was so frank
and generous, so jovial and cordial, so genial and kind,
and withal so manly and high toned, and so familiar with
the duties of his station, that you were ready to give him
your hand and heart in return for his, which he seemed
ever ready to proffer. He was then in the heyday of
popularity, and appeared to be the owner of the talisman
that secured for him the choicest favors of fortune, and he
was characterized as her most lucky pet. I have always
noticed that when men are either petted by the people, or
have what is called a continuous run of good luck, that
they generally possess the mental and personal qualities
that justify the petting, and the judgment and prudence to
secure the successes they win.

 During Mr. Tyler's gubernatorial term, he was elected
to the senate of the United States, and while in that body
was chosen president of the senate, to preside during the
temporary absence of the vice president, and no man who
ever occupied the station of senator gave his mind and
strength to the service of the state with more devotion and
love. He was a strict constructionist of the old school,
and had been brought up to admire and to carry out the
principles inculcated in Madison's report. Throughout his
whole course in the senate he never swerved for a moment
from the most rigid interpretation of the constitution, and
from the most strict limitation of executive power; and
notwithstanding these were his avowed and well understood opinions, and had been acted upon with the utmost
firmness in all the public trusts with which he had been
invested, yet, after his retirement from the senate, he was
selected by the Whig party as its candidate for the office of

vice president, and was elected, and as is well known, by the death of the president in one month after entering upon the office, he became the president, and served out his official term. It is easy to understand how, under such circumstances, he became unpopular with the Democratic party, and was denounced by them. And then when he began to act upon the principles in which he was nurtured, which had become a second nature to him, and with the firmness and resolution of his character began to veto the long-cherished measures of the party which had elected him, and to control their action, it is perfectly natural that he should have become distasteful to them. Of course, popular favor deserted him for a time, and he was the subject of bitter vituperation and of acrimonious feeling for the greater portion of his administration. But when he summoned around him as members of his cabinet such men as John C. Calhoun, and Abel P. Upshur, and Thomas W. Gilmer, and John Y. Mason, and Hugh S. Legare, men of exalted talents, of high-toned character and virtues, of upright honesty and deserved popularity, the genial warmth of other days began to revive, party asperity began to be mellowed and softened, and long before his death he was again beloved, and was held in high estimation as a virtuous patriot.

And when stormy times came round again, when the southern states had been roused by sectional strife and threatened oppression, by violations of the constitution, and impending violations of the rights of property, to dissolve the Union, and had formed another government, Mr. Tyler was summoned from his retirement and elected a member of the convention of Virginia to consider whether she should unite her fortunes with the new Confederacy. Virginia, as is well known, paused long, and was willing to make every effort to save the Union. Mr. Tyler was appointed one of the commissioners to attempt to reconcile the contending sections, and prevent, if possible, the threatened war. We know the fate of his mission. We know,

4

on his return, he counselled a severance of the Union, and that Virginia took her place with her southern sisters. We know that he became a member of the Confederate congress, and that all his powers were exerted in the cause of the Confederacy. With heart and soul he lent his energies and faculties to rouse and encourage the people, to infuse vigor and life into the public councils, to energize the decimated ranks of our armies, and uphold our gallant officers and noble defenders. And we know the sad result.

In all these situations Mr. Tyler was the same resolute and firm representative, the same sincere and devoted patriot, and the same warm and kind friend. He commenced his career as a member of the house of delegates at the age of one and twenty, and as soon as he was eligible, was elected a representative in the congress of the United States, and being thus, from boyhood, in all the most elevated public positions, he was thoroughly familiar with all the men of note, and perfectly versed in all the great measures which had agitated and controlled the councils of the state and the nation. His father before him had been governor of the state, and wherever the old blood is traced it is the progenitor of noble and virtuous actions. Mr. Tyler's remains were deposited in Hollywood cemetery by the side of the ashes of Monroe. Let these two bright jewels be placed in the same casket, and let affection gather around and perform the office of keeping up their beauty and brilliance.

My friends, we have all seen some lovely bride in her bridal robes, the emblem of purity, with a flowing veil partly concealing, partly exhibiting her modest features, gathered in folds about her brow by a brooch of pearls clustering to form a beautiful laurel bud, all to shed a mild glory around her graceful form. Such a picture reminds me of Virginia in her maiden bloom, with her sons clustering around her like bees about their queen, forming a brooch worthy to adorn the brow of any bridal state. Such sons as Randolph, of Roanoke, and Littleton W. Tazewell, and

Wm. B. Giles, and Benj. W. Leigh, Chapman Johnson, Abel P. Upshur, James Barbour, Philip P. Barbour, Robert B. Taylor, William S. Archer and John W. Jones, and I could give you a more extended catalogue, brighter and nobler than those which Homer gives of his warriors gathered around the walls of Troy. But who can do justice to such men as these; who can do himself justice, or do honor to the country that gave them birth, by attempting to give an inkling of their histories, a surface view of their characters, or a shadow of the circumstances by which they were environed. I am skimming along like a swallow on the surface of a meadow, and can only give you a faint idea of the style of oratory of some of them as it appeared to me when I have hung upon the inspirations that dropped from their tongues.

I invoke my memory, unaided by books or documents, to bring before you a reminiscence of Randolph of Roanoke—one of the most remarkable men of this or of any age. The whole appearance of the man was striking. His head, in proportion to his frame, was small, his hair, which he parted in the middle, grew low upon his brow, and contradicted the science of phrenologists, by giving to one with an expanded brain and great mind a remarkably low forehead; his features were rather delicate and feminine, and gave him the appearance, when he first went to congress, of extreme youth, which induced the speaker, when he was about to administer to him his official oath, to enquire if he had attained the constitutional age, and which elicited from his ever ready tongue the response, "Go ask my constituents." His eyes were black and full of lustre, his voice peculiarly feminine and shrill, yet clear as the tones of a silver bell, and he could give it a compass which would enable the hearer at a distance to catch his lowest whisper, when he assayed the deep or the pathetic. His neck was very short, and deeply seated between his shoulders, which were somewhat elevated; the frame of his body, for one so thin, was massive, his arms unusually

long, and his fingers attenuated, and when he extended
that right arm in debate, and shook that dexter finger, it
gave you an idea of the warnings and threatenings that
were to follow; his limbs, from his body downwards, were
long and thin, and made him much taller than he seemed
while seated.   His dress at times was fantastic, at one time
appearing in a full jockey suit, jockey cap, roundabout,
long top boots as high as his knees, spurs and whip like
one equipped for a race; at another time wrapped in Rus-
sian furs, from his cap to his feet; and then again in plain
attire, such as other gentlemen wore who are best dressed,
when the habiliments attract least notice—simple, be-
coming and appropriate to the man, the place and the
occasion.

I heard him twice in debate, once in the senate of the
United States as the compeer of Calhoun and of Webster,
and the antagonist of Clay.   When I heard him the first
time he was in one of his excited moods, when his brain
seemed to be charged with electricity, and the sparkles
flew around him as heated metal throws off corruscations
when struck by some vulcan's hammer.   His style was
eccentric, rapidly jumping from subject to subject like
meteors flying from a common centre, and you would have
thought from his sharp hits, right and left, that he would
strike some of the great spheres revolving there, and hurl
them beneath his feet.   Like Phæton driving the coursers
of the sun, with magic power he would smoothly and ma-
jestically glide up the ascent of the blue firmament, and
then again suddenly, with impetuous daring, dash along,
seeming to have lost all control of himself, his coursers or
his chariot, and all regard for his appointed track.   He
would seem to lose sight of the subject in debate, and to
be hunting his game in out of the way places, but before
you were aware of his object, you would hear his double
barrel in the midst of a whole covey, and he invariably
bagged the bird at which he fired.   With all this there
were connecting links of argument and illustration,

pointed and glaring, when the application of his eccentricities was made manifest. Senators laid down their pens, and turned with eager eyes full upon him, and auditors stood breathless until he paused, then expanded their lungs with a full inhalation, and listened with profound attention for another outpouring.

I heard him again in 1829–'30 in the convention. I think I see him now as he stood before me then. The question for discussion was whether white population and taxation combined should be the basis of representation. There was a large old stove, of the colonial times, which then heated the hall, having the arms of the colony cast in the metal, with the motto, "*En dat Virginia quartem.*" Mr. Randolph had a few days before called my attention to it, and said he revered it for its antiquity, the hand of innovation had not reached it, and it made Virginia the fourth estate in the realm. From this stove a pipe ran into the opposite partition, and a plain staff which could be grasped with the hand arose from the floor and supported this pipe. Whether he had taken the position because he desired the support of something that had the appearance of stability I know not; but when he rose, he grasped and supported himself by this staff with his left hand, his right arm being free. It was late in the day, and the concourse of people who usually attended the debates had nearly all dispersed. But in less time than I could conceive it possible for the information to have been carried, every avenue to the room was flooded, and men walked on tiptoe, as if afraid that the creaking of their shoes might lose them a single word. His manner was entirely different from that I have heretofore attempted to describe. It was calm, collected, dignified and commanding, and his gesticulation was that of a master actor. He would begin to express a thought in language, and then leaving the sentence incomplete, would by a wave of the hand, or a change of the muscles of the face, give the idea as perfect to the mind as if conveyed by the most speaking words. No reporter can catch these peculiarities, and it is difficult to convey a just conception of the effect. He went on smoothly, expressing his astonishment at the changes that had been proposed to the constitution, that no part of it should be left untouched, expressed his amazement at such a result, believed it was the very best constitution, not for Japan, not for China, not for New England, or for old England, but for this our ancient commonwealth of Virginia. I remember one thought, and his manner of uttering it: "I am unwilling to pull down the edifice of our state government from the garret to the cellar; aye, down to the foundation stone." And then he said, "The gentleman from Augusta," and he seized his cravat with both hands, and twisted and pulled at it, as if feeling a sense of extreme suffocation, and the contortions of face united with the efforts of the hands to relax the throttle he felt, the whole gesture expressing the idea so forcibly, that you saw it palpable that he intended to say that Virginia was suffering strangulation from the ruffians who were assailing her. And yet he went on with another idea. These things must be seen to be understood. No man that ever I have seen equalled him in this respect. He took up the great subject before the convention, and argued it with power, grouping the arguments of his opponents, and turning them with force against them. I remember one other thought. He said he had been told not to look at the federal government. And this in Virginia, " where to use a very homely phrase, but one that exactly suits the case, we can't take a step without breaking our shins over some federal obstacle." Mr. Randolph's style was not that of a close reasoner, of one who lays his premises at a distance, and then step by step advances to the conclusion. It was disjointed, not dove-tailed, but when fully and spiritedly presented as he did it, it was equally overwhelming.

Mr. Randolph was a descendant through his father from Pocahontas, the daughter of Powhatan, the great Indian chief. He was elected a member of the house of representatives in 1799, and was in that body twenty-six years. He was in the senate of the United States for two years, and was then elected a member of the convention of Virginia. After the adjournment of the convention, General Jackson appointed him minister plenipotentiary to Russia. He died in Philadelphia on the 24th of May, 1833.

What would he have thought if he had lived to the present day? What would have been the thoughts of all the men of whom I have spoken? How would they have acted had they been on the arena of Virginia now? Not only to see the constitution of their fathers disowned and disavowed, but to see the men of the present day living under a *thing* called a constitution adopted by a miserable set of a *wretched* minority of three or four counties of this old commonwealth, the "*magna mater virum*," and those counties under the thraldom of military occupation, sending forth spawn, to rule and have dominion over her people! What would these men think were they here now, when literally we cannot take a step without breaking our shins over some federal obstacle? It might have been tolerated when military satraps held the sway and supported the ill-gotten power by the bayonet and the shell. It might have been tolerated when a military commander could veto your laws, unrebuked even by a mild remonstrance, and could say to the people of this city you may elect whom you please as your mayor, but if you elect a man distasteful to me he shall not serve. It might have been tolerated when your sons were in prison, and you spake with bated breath lest the dungeon should be your portion. But when peace has been proclaimed, and you are allowed to have a legislature of your own, is there no remedy? If the faintest semblance of self-government remains, if there is any power residing in the people to do anything, they might call a convention to wipe from existence the incubus; that is, the ever-rising, never-ending remembrancer of degradation, and having been born again, begin the new life with old principles, but with a

new constitution and new men. They might in the new
organic law bring to a full stop the existence of the as-
sumed power of those who, from the honorable position to
which they have been improperly elevated, can recommend
an amendment to the federal constitution, which I am
proud to see the general assembly of this state has indig-
nantly rejected; by which every Virginian, who deserves
the name, would humble and debase himself in his own
eyes, and in the estimation of every honorable man, if he
could vote for it; by which Virginia would be required
to degrade her highest and noblest worthies; by which
she would consent forever to disfranchise Robert E. Lee,
and the men who stood shoulder to shoulder and upheld
his arms in the grand and matchless defence of the ever-
renowned capitol of his honored state; by which she
would discard and disinherit the Stonewall brigade, and
the friends and compatriots of the lion-hearted Jackson—

> "The legions who had seen his glance
>   Across the carnage flashing,
> And thrilled to catch his ringing "*charge*"
>   Above the volley crashing;"

by which she would renounce the men who rode trium-
phant with the "wings of the army," the cavalry of
Stuart; by which the veterans, whose hearts never felt a
quail, should be scouted from your councils; by which
you would elevate and honor ignorant Africans, and dis-
honor and disgrace the men who were spurring by the side
of "Ashby, our Paladin," to

> "Catch the last words of cheer
>   Dropped from his tongue!
> Over the volleys din
>   Let them be rung!
>
> "Follow me! follow me!!"
>   Soldier! oh! could there be
> Pæan or dirge for thee
>   Loftier sung."

If we have not the power to get rid of even the Alexandria constitution and its representatives, then fold the
arms in solemn pride, and let them do their worst.

I return from this digression and come back to the pearls
of great price. I hope you will bear with me while I attempt to draw a faint sketch of another orator whom I
think one of the most gifted of our Virginia statesmen. I
allude to Abel P. Upshur, a jurist, a judge, a representative, a member of the convention of 1829–'30, secretary of
the navy and secretary of state during the administration
of Mr. Tyler. His forte, I think, was in a deliberative
assembly. I heard him on many occasions at the bar, for
he was for a long period attorney for the commonwealth
in this city. I have listened to his lucid, short, distinct
and able opinions delivered off hand as a judge. I wit-
nessed some of his efforts in the convention; but the most
powerful speech of his life, that I know of, was delivered
in the house of delegates on the proposition to repeal the
law which prohibited a man from marrying his wife's
sister. Judge Upshur was of large frame, broad shoulders,
expanded chest, fine head, high and capacious forehead, as
if the brain had pressed it outward. It was like the massive brow of Daniel Webster, though his eyebrows did not
throw the dark shade upon the face that Webster's did,
but there was a sunshine playing upon the features as if
the light had been reflected from his exceeding bald head.
One eye was defective, but the other was so speaking, that
it threw the defective one in the shade. At that time old
General Samuel Blackburn was a member from the county
of Bath. He was a remarkable man, too, in his day, was
a grim, morose old customer, who had a peculiar intellect
of his own, which displayed uncommon powers, but delighted most in cutting hits upon his brother members, and
his blows had been given so hard, and repeated so often,
that he became a terror to the young, and the older avoided
encounters with him. He had never failed to turn the
laugh upon his antagonists, and made them subjects of his

5

ridicule and mirth. Judge Upshur had delivered a master effort in favor of the bill before the house, and when he concluded, having delighted all beyond measure, and the effect was manifest in the beaming of the countenances of the audience, and in the quivering tear that hung on the undried lid, and which rough men were ashamed to wipe away, lest they might unfold their weakness, General Blackburn undertook to dispel the illusion, and by the employment of his old weapons to break the force of the argument. He let slip all his dogs, and attempted to worry the game by snapping and barking, but as long as he confined himself to howlings at arguments which were untouched and unimpaired, a playful smile only lighted up the judge's face; but at length he took another tack, and assailed his personal appearance, and drew upon his fancy for imaginings, derogatory to his personal character, and he assayed to laugh him to scorn, and throw him into contempt. Then I saw the great man's bosom heave, and his countenance seemed to grow radiant with a glow, the inspiration of the orator filled his soul. "When Achilles was about to draw his sword against Agamemnon, his king and chief, we are told the blue-eyed goddess suddenly stood behind him with terrible look, invisible to every one but himself, seized his yellow hair, and assuaged the wrath of the young hero with prudent advice. He withdrew his mighty hand from the silver handle, and the sword dropped back into the scabbard." Not so Upshur; the blue-eyed Pallas lent him the Egis of Jove, and he shook its flaming boss full in the eyes of all the house. He began with tones that moved the hair on your head, and told that his blood was up. He was calm as he is who in danger knows no fear—with measured step, and slow, he stalked along, and he balanced his words in his hands to see that they were well chosen and of the proper weight. There was a solemnity around that you could feel; he kept removing the little impediments from his path, and as he advanced he grew "warm, energetic, chaste, sublime," and when at last he had acquired the proper pitch, and felt the key-note had roused his brain, he turned upon the foe,

> " And, with a withering look,
> The war-denouncing trumpet took,"

and his words hissed and scorched. And then he left, as it seemed, the hateful theme, and he would come back to the subject in debate, and with a mellowed voice soft tones were dropped, as if the lighter shades were thrown in to make the darkness gloomy and the night more black, and then he would serenely recall the imputations on his person and character that had roused his ire, and assuming the tones with which he first began, he drove right onward, "and still he kept his wild, unaltered mien, while each strained ball of sight seemed bursting from his head."

I never shall forget that day. I never shall forget the look of the denounced and discomfited assailant. I never shall cease to remember the spell that bound the hearers, and how men gave expression to their feelings by pressing around the speaker when he concluded, and giving him the cordial grip of the sympathetic hand. Such is a faint effort to give you some idea of the manner of the roused and animated Upshur.

I would wish to tell of all the jewels I have mentioned, but time will not allow. There are other gems to constitute the valued ornaments for Virginia's person. I can only name the bright list of her governors in my day, whose persons are familiar to my memory as the Lares and Penates of an ancient household, many of whom have been intimate and personal friends, whose inestimable worth I have seen tried in that hard test of merit, the alembic of party feeling and party vituperation, and who have come out of the contest like pebbles from the depths of ocean, whiter and more polished by the very agitation of the waters in which they have been revolving.

Of Wm. H. Cabell and James Barbour, Wilson Cary Nicholas, James P. Preston, Thomas Mann Randolph and

James Pleasants, my father's associates, boon companions and bosom friends, who came to his house in social intercourse, and indulged in the pleasantries of unreserved, unrestrained conversation, interchanging frequent, rich and intellectual repasts.

I have heard them reading over the rough drafts of their messages, intended for the general assembly, and listened to his and their comments, and caught from them the ardent desire so frequently expressed, to do something to develop the resources, protect the interests, and defend and maintain the rights of their native state—to educate the minds, and build up the fortunes of the humble among her citizens—to establish, adorn and fructify Virginia through all her borders.

And from the commencement of my official career to its termination, I can only mention, with high respect and esteem, the names of William B. Giles, John Floyd, Littleton W. Tazewell, David Campbell, Thomas W. Gilmer, James McDowell, William Smith, John B. Floyd, Joseph Johnson, Henry A. Wise and John Letcher; and her acting governors, Wyndham Robertson, John M. Patton, John Rutherfoord and John M. Gregory. What a space in the eyes of the nation have not these men filled? How dear have they been in the just affections of the people. How ardently they too strove to elevate the name of Virginia. How they gloried in endeavoring to save the Union by preserving the constitution, straining every nerve to check the unlimited exercise of ungranted powers, and to restrain the different departments of the government within their respective spheres, uttering continued warnings and thrilling appeals to prevent sectional jealousies and sectional strife, and foreshadowing with gloomy forebodings the gathering storm, while they solemnly and ardently hoped for the preservation of peace. God, in his wisdom, willed it otherwise; brothers' hands have been imbued with brothers' blood, and woe, with unnumbered ills, has followed in the wake of desolating war. How sad it is to

look over the bright catalogue, and note how few there are
who have not gone to the silent tomb; and though

> " Their fame on brightest pages,
> Penned by poets and by sages,
> Shall go sounding through the ages ;"

yet the very monuments that were reared to honor their
names have been torn from the state and obliterated from
her record. Oh! it was thought that if a portion of Virginia's territory should bear their honored names, it would
be a monument more enduring than marble or bronze ; but
it has been reserved for him who occupies that executive
chair, that each of them graced and adorned, to perpetrate
the deed, and to have been one of the foremost to obliterate
our ancient boundaries, and to give the counties that bore
their names to a bastard state. Better that they should
have " been cold and dead, and lying low," than to have
heard " the wailing of our people in their woe." Shame
on the sons of the state who aided in accomplishing the
deed. Shame on the men of the nation who ratified the
outrage. Shame on the men

> "Who would have our proud eagle to feed on the eyes
> Of those who have taught him so grandly to soar."

I can barely allude to the long list of her judges. Her
revered, honored, simple hearted, learned Marshall, her
Wythe and Pendleton, her Tuckers—I could dwell upon
this name and his exalted worth—her Roane, Brooke, Carr,
Cabell, Coalter, Daniel, Brockenbrough and Stanard. Justice, according to the ancient poets, was depicted with a
bandage over her eyes, indicating that she could not be
impartial unless deprived of her sight. Such men as these,
with eyes unfettered, and with minds unbiassed by passion
or prejudice, could hold the scales of justice with even
balance, and dispense her fair and equitable judgments
without exciting a murmur of discontent. Their opinions
were everywhere received as sound and true interpretations

of the subtleties of law and of constitutional right. Can
you imagine anything more abhorrent to the feelings of
such men, thus versed in constitutions and laws, and in the
principles of free government, as adopted and adored until
now by the people in every state in the Union, than to see
the military superior to the civil power, and contemning
and controlling its judges after a proclamation of peace,
denying the writ of habeas corpus, and petty military commanders refusing to obey it. Judges lending themselves
to the dirty work of packing juries, and suborning and
paying witnesses to testify falsely against the purest and
best men in the land. Aye, judges confiscating property,
and rendering judgments in their own favor, to secure that
property for themselves. Denying the representative of a
brave and noble people, who had been insulted, manacled
and confined in the unwholesome cell of a dungeon, in the
strongest fort in the world, the right to know the offence
for which he was incarcerated, to be confronted with his
accusers, and the right to a speedy trial by an impartial
jury—a right secured in the constitution to the meanest
person accused of any offence—a right which the great
men of Virginia and of every other state declared to "per-
tain to them and their posterity as the basis and foundation of government." What would such men as Marshall,
and Wythe, and Roane have said, if they had been asked
by a committee of congress if they could procure a jury
in their courts to convict a criminal? I can imagine the
look from the flashing eye of the old chief justice. It
would have indicated that he felt the question was an in-
sult, and he would have retorted that Virginia judges never
packed juries at the bidding of any authority for any purpose. He would have added, that no man who had the
character to be summoned on a jury could be found who
would act if he had made up his mind to convict any pri-
soner, and that the judge who would instruct the sheriff to
summon a jury for such a purpose, would be as base as the
juror who would do his bidding. Such would be the lan-

guage of any man worthy to be a judge. He would sooner rest with the blessed, until

> " The last and dreadful hour
> This crumbling pageant shall devour,"

than be the hateful instrument to execute a hateful purpose by corrupt means of degrading a proud and great man who has become the very embodiment of a proud and grand people. Corruption may do its worst, but fetters and dungeons cannot bind the soul or disturb the mind conscious of rectitude and glorying in virtue. Such judges as these, though, would have rejoiced to see that the supreme court have at last had the firmness to throw themselves into the breach, and to decide that the military must be subservient to the civil power, and that no more trials of civilians shall be permitted before military tribunals on any pretence whatever. With such decisions as those we may say, there is a department where justice and right predominate, and there is a spark of the old fire kindling on liberty's altar. Perchance it may burn pure and bright as in other days.

Few men in any government have had a finer opportunity to learn the capacities, the feelings and principles which actuate the mind and elucidate the character of public men than I have had while seated at the humble desk in the legislative and executive halls of the state for the last forty years. But why do I call it humble, when the office of the clerk of the house of delegates has been occupied by such men as Edmund Randolph, George Wythe, William Wirt, James Pleasants, William Munford, St. George Tucker and William F. Gordon, men of far-reaching intellects and exalted virtues. By Randolph, the first attorney-general of the state, and the first attorney-general of the United States, who had been a member of congress, governor, secretary of state under General Washington, and member of the conventions which adopted and ratified the constitution of the United States. By Wythe, the pure and virtuous chancellor, who had been in the house of burgesses, member of the convention, member of congress, signer of the declaration of independence, speaker of the house of delegates, judge of the court of appeals, member of the conventions on the constitution of the United States, revisor of the state laws, professor of law at William and Mary college, and a philosopher, instilling into the minds of his pupils principles of virtue and wisdom. By Wirt, the chaste, refined and eloquent orator, chancellor, district attorney, and attorney-general of the United States. And by Pleasants, distinguished for high public and private virtues, who had been member of congress, United States senator, governor, member of the convention of 1829–'30, and was twice appointed judge, but modestly declined to serve from a distrust of his own qualifications—a distrust which no one entertained but himself. To chancellor Wythe was reserved the honor of devising the emblems and motto for the seal of the state. On one side were *Libertas, Ceres, Eternitas,* with the motto, *Perseverando.* The blessings of liberty and abundance for eternity were to be obtained by perseverance. On the other side, Virtus with her foot upon the tyrant's neck, and the motto, "*Sic semper tyrannis.*" But it was reserved for the wiseacres at Wheeling, or the literati at Alexandria, or the officers of those governments, I cannot discover which, to change this remnant of antiquity, and to mar the unity of these thoughts by crowding into the seal the motto, "Liberty and Union." *Libertas* with her cap and pileus, was not liberty enough for those who were destroying the liberty of the white race, so they inserted liberty again. And they added the word Union as entirely appropriate, because the state was not in the Union at the time; and the same men deny her admission now. Liberty abridged, and Union disunited. For eighty-three years the old seal was deemed good enough for Virginia. If I had the power I would obliterate the new motto as one of the first acts connected with the restitution of the state to vindicate the intellects of her great men, and the authority of her first convention. Let the seal of George Wythe remain unblurred by the Alexandria usurpation. When the old state shall be razeed into a territory, let them blur the seal to their heart's content—its emblems and mottoes will be inappropriate then. Let some representative of the Alexandria convention haul down the old flag from the capitol and throw it into the garret. But you can never erase from the soul of an old-fashioned Virginian the burning desire to see Virtus with her foot upon the tyrant's neck :

"You may break, you may shatter the vase if you will,
But the scent of the roses will hang round it still."

The greater the oppression, the greater the tyranny—the more glorious will the old motto be.

I have been told that the last legislature recognized this interpolation upon the seal, by enacting that the seal now in possession of the secretary of the commonwealth should continue to be the seal of the state. If that seal was adopted without a shadow of authority, as I believe is the fact, I do hope the act will be repealed, and the old seal revived.

, It is a great pleasure to me sometimes to look back into the past and pleasantly to recall the men of other days with whom I have been associated; and there is no reminiscence more delightful than the intercourse I have had with the various speakers of the house of delegates whom I have known, or under whom I have served—men of whom any state might be proud. Such men as James Barbour, Andrew Stevenson, Robert Stanard, Linn Banks, Joel Holleman, Thomas W. Gilmer, George W. Hopkins, William O. Goode and Valentine W. Southall—men who were deeply versed in parliamentary lore, and understood the advantage of a rigid application of simple but wise rules for the government of assemblies. In those days there was comparatively little necessity for the speaker's gavel to command order. There was something in the richness and mellow tones of old James Barbour's voice—

6

something in the commanding, and I may say domineering manner of Andrew Stevenson—something in the firm, sharp and decisive way of Linn Banks, and in the decorum and dignity of each, that generated dignity and decorum in all around. There was no confusion, business was expedited, system and order prevailed, and the house of delegates of Virginia was a model for deliberative assemblies. In those days I have seen old Peter Francisco, the giant sergeant-at-arms, so renowned in revolutionary times for his herculean strength, grasp a stout man by the collar with his left hand, and raising him from the floor with perfect ease, walk him out of the house for having improperly intruded within the bar. There was no necessity to direct such a sergeant to preserve order in the lobby. But these men are all gone. I can only say now, twine laurel wreaths around their graves, sprinkle orange blossoms over their ashes, let them linger in your memories, and spring up in sempiternal verdure in the gardens where trees of life will flourish.

And there is no recollection more agreeable than the intellectual repasts I have had while witnessing the effects of oratory when handled by a skillful master. It is gratifying to view the power of the human mind upon other minds—to see how the master plays upon the strings of sympathy—how his reason convinces the judgment of others—how he animates, refreshes, instructs—how an assembly will be swayed to and fro as an earthquake makes the mountains reel. I have seen such effects produced by the inspirations of the Prestons and McDowell, by Henry A. Wise, Joseph C. Cabell, and Charles Fenton Mercer, and the Masons, and the brilliant and impetuous Dromgoole, and Robert E. Scott, and R. M. T. Hunter, and Gholson, and Brodnax, and the Robertsons, and Flournoy, and Edmunds, and John Thompson Brown, the bright and morning star. Men who would have graced any station—men with brilliant genius and erudition, with the *amor patriæ* warm in their hearts, and glowing and passionate expressions of filial piety to Virginia dropping from their tongues—men who had imbibed their ideas of government from the fathers of the revolution, and would have scouted and scorned the political vagaries, and heresies, and radical rabies of the present day—men who, like Dromgoole, could ride on the whirlwind and direct the storm, or who, like John Thompson Brown, with plaintive voice and dulcet tones, seemed to be dipping his fingers in purest water, and drawing forth melody from the gentle vibrations of musical glasses.

While my theme confines me to Virginia's jewels, and I have therefore mentioned none others, yet I am not limited to the boundaries of the state, and if time would permit, I would open caskets full of bright ornaments. Such men as William Henry Harrison and Zachary Taylor, presidents of the United States, military gems, endowed with gold medals, emblazoned with emblems and devices of victories and gallant triumphs. Virginia rocked them in her cradle, and dandled them on her knee; their honors are her honors, and history has recorded and etched their achievements into the very memory of mankind; and Henry Clay, the glorious old orator and patriot, whose fame is as undying as any of them; and William H. Crawford, and William C. Preston, and John S. Preston, and John J. Crittenden, and Sterling Price; and I could surround their names with governors of other states, senators and representatives, cabinet ministers, foreign ambassadors, officers of the army and navy, judges and professors, bishops and clergy, authors, historians and poets, who have proudly claimed Virginia as their native land, and filled their high offices with honor to themselves and advantage to their fellow-men.

And besides all these there are jewels of the public press, that great power in free government that cannot be overlooked, whose wheels, like Ezekiel's vision of the cherubims, are instinct with eyes to enable them to discover what is passing, and with wings spreading in every direction to carry information with the rapidity of the wind. Among these I can but mention Thomas Ritchie, the old Napoleon of the press, and John Hampden Pleasants, the Javelin to pierce, and the keen-edged sword to cut and to slash, and O. Jennings Wise, the hero of Roanoke island, as bright with the pen as with the sword.

Swiftly hurrying on as I am, I can only say for the gems that have been omitted, go look in your country's pages, you will find them there, sparkling like "the stars which glitter in the noon of night;" and I can imagine that all the stars in the heavens are but the mild and speaking eyes of Virginia's sons, looking down with smiles upon their mother—smiling, because invested with power to see that the dark shadow which at present eclipses her once radiant disk will pass away, and her light will shine again in accustomed splendor.

If you will bear with me a little longer, I am coming down to later times, when the usurpations of the federal government, prophesied or foreshadowed by our fathers, caused the southern states to attempt to assume among the powers of the earth a separate and independent station. I am coming down rapidly to the time when Virginia, feeling these usurpations as either immediate, or threatened as ultimately certain, assembled her other memorable convention, and having exhausted all powers of conciliation, and used all proper and jealous precautions, united her fate with that of her southern sisters. It was the power she interposed between the government and the other states that made her soil the chief battleground of the dreadful contest, and brought upon her desolation and anguish. It was her devotion to the cause that impelled her to throw wide open the doors of her treasury, and devote all her finances to the accomplishment of the common purpose—to throw open her arsenals, and dedicate all her military stores and great resources to the common defence—to bring forward her priceless jewels, her peerless sons, and bid them offer in her name their glorious services, and lay down, if need be, their valued lives to vindicate a people's honor. Nothing did she withhold—all was perilled. Everything was absolutely sacrificed. And this is the reason to-day that she is at the mercy of those who know no mercy, and is bereft of her rights by those who have no magnanimity in their souls. But though we are thus bereft, we have yet the poor privilege of returning "thanks to-day, that neither our terrible sufferings, nor the abuse of our enemies, have converted us into base poltroons, nor taught us to heap dust and ashes upon the history, memories and traditions of the joys and sorrows of our grand but fruitless struggle for national independence."

And while hope seems hopeless, we have learned a lesson of patient endurance, and been taught that we must wait until those who are now revelling with the strong and aiding the mighty, shall themselves feel the grasp of the wrongdoer, and have their rights wrested from them, and shall see the necessity of peacefully applying some remedy other than that to which we resorted with all the power that God had given us.

These were trying times, when the assembled congress of the Confederacy pondered over the affairs of the unrecognized nation. When all the nations of the earth were looking on at the fearful fray, and while in their hearts they could not but applaud the noble resistance we were making, yet coldly threw every obstacle in our way, and permitted their hundreds of thousands to swell the million against us, and gave us the neutrality that benefitted the United States alone. Oh! those were trying times, when our Randolph and Seddon in the cabinet—our Hunter and Preston and Caperton in the senate, and our Tyler and Rives and Bocock and Lyons and Baldwin and Brockenbrough, Russell, Preston, Johnston, Goode, Garnett and Chambliss and others were, day by day and night after night, encouraging and strengthening the national arm : and though differing as to the best course, and objecting often to the policy pursued, yet ever demonstrating that, let who would falter, Virginia was steadfast in her resolution, and would maintain her faith to the utmost extremity. No man in that assembly or elsewhere, when he talked of failures or losses, or submission, could point the finger at Virginia and say, "You did it." When she failed, it was after a desperate struggle. When she encountered losses, they were accompanied by four-fold losses to the enemy, that made him stagger and reel. When submission came, it was the submission of all; but she was there, if possible to avert it—overwhelmed, not dismayed. When hope fled affrighted and desolation reigned supreme, she was there to bear the brunt.

My friends—I cannot quit my exhaustless theme, without pausing for a moment to bestow one grateful acknowledgment to those who survive this dreadful ruin—one tearful eulogium upon those who gave their lives in the fruitless endeavor to redeem their country from degradation and oppression. I would I could dwell upon the brilliant achievements of our noble armies, and the personal daring of their great commanders. I would I could record all the glories that glittered around our handful of famous but unfortunate ships, and that decked the brows of their intrepid officers. I can barely recite the names of a few of Virginia's warriors, and must leave it to our sister states to perpetuate the memories of their heroes and patriots. I must leave the record to be illustrated and graven in never-dying measures, by the Homers and Shakespeares who shall spring from the halls of our literary institutions, where moral grandeur shall be taught by the greatest of those heroes and patriots. I must leave to some gifted orator, with his soul elevated by the inspiration of a Randolph, an Upshur or a Wise, to pour forth eulogies in their praise, so exalted that "the world should listen then as I am listening now." I can only recall the bright list of names, and bid you recall the devotion you felt towards them when they rode upon their war steeds, with small, compact and intrepid bands of soldiers near them, and the once proud banner floating o'er them.

> " For though conquered, you adore it;
> Love the cold, dead hands that bore it,
> And weep for those who fell before it."

Names of Robert E. Lee and Joseph E. Johnston and Thomas J. Jackson and Early and Stuart and Ashby and the Lees and Rosser and Beverley Robertson and Thomas T. Munford, Ewell, Armistead, Magruder, Hill, the Joneses, Rhodes, Wise, Floyd and Taliaferro, Pendleton, Mahone, Anderson, Kemper, Pryor, Corse, Pegram, Imboden, Heth, Garnett, Edward Johnson, Lomax, Mosby, Hunton and Smith, and Allen, Preston, Cummings, Harris, Echols, Cocke, Gibbons, Garland, Walker, Terry, Brockenbrough.

Oh! how their bright faces are cherished in the albums of our memories; how the incidents of their lives are garnered among our treasures; how we pity the unknown private, as he passes by with his sleeveless arm, or his single leg, hobbling on his crutch—unknown, but honored in our hearts; how the youths and the boys hang upon the recital of all their glories; how the faded uniforms will be hung up and preserved; and the very buttons that clasped their bosoms will become precious keepsakes and amulets. Power may endeavor to secrete them, by meanly cutting them from the coat of one who from his poverty had nothing else to wear, but they will be hid among the trinkets of our maidens, and be wept over by mothers as relics of a dying son; and the button from the coat of Lee or of Jackson will in after time be purchased in other climes, where greatness is admired, as priceless mementoes. Men will cherish the memories and traditions of the wounded, and the immortal dead who perished in what they believed a holy cause. They cannot forget their own rejoicings and cheerings for victories, nor the sorrows and moanings for the defeats of our harassed, outnumbered and overpowered veterans. They will not forget the purity of our women, nor the sacrifices they made, nor the works of their hands, nor their ministrations to the sick, the wounded and the dying, nor their animating presence, the wave of the parting hand, nor the cheer of their excited voices rousing the sinking spirit in time of gloom, and encouraging their loved ones to daring and peril for the sake of country.

Oh, we cannot dwell upon them now, but we will never forget, and they cannot tear from our thoughts the history and the glorious traditions of Manassas, of Kernstown, Cross Keys, Port Republic, Front Royal, Alleghany, Winchester, Cedar Creek, of Williamsburg and Fredericksburg, Chancellorsville, Seven Pines, Harpers' Ferry, Sharpsburg, Boonsborough, Antietam, Middletown, and Gettysburg, and Chickahominy, Mechanicsville, Ellyson's Mills, Beaver Dam Creek, Gaines' Mill, Cold Harbour, Garnett's farm, Malvern Hill, Drewrys' Bluff and Petersburg—nor Roanoke Island, nor Donelson, nor Shiloh, nor Vicksburg, nor Chickamauga, nor Pea Ridge, nor Charleston, nor the mighty struggles over mountain and valley, moor and hill from the Potomac to the Rio Grande.

But I weary you with my long detail. The glories of these fields in this day need no description. And though the Southern Confederacy has gone down never to rise, and her name is not among the list of nations, she will be like the sun when he sets—whose "glory remains when his light fades away." Oh, we can no more see her armies battling for right and astonishing the world; we can no more see her spotless banner waving over her ramparts; we can no more rally her men, or inspire breath into her dry bones that she may live. We must acquiesce in the hard necessity that is upon us—droop our hopes and enfold our conquered cause in our hearts, and

"Furl that banner, for 'tis weary,
Round its staff 'tis drooping dreary.
 Furl it—fold it; it is best;
For there 's not a man to wave it,
And there 's not a sword to save it;—

There 's not one left to lave it
In the blood that heroes gave it ;—
And its foes *now* scorn and brave it !
Furl it—fold it; let it rest !"

There is a duty which we still have to perform, a debt of gratitude which we must pay. Our southern wives and daughters have inaugurated the undertaking and it is glorious to follow in their lead. They have collected the bones of the mighty dead and furled the banner around them; they have gathered the ashes into urns and placed them among the monuments and cenotaphs of the cemetery, and it is their purpose to beautify and adorn the place so that pilgrims may come to it as a modern Mecca. They purpose to perform the duty of keeping the graves clear of the damp and noxious weed, to freshen and chisel deeper the names and the epitaphs on the simple tombs affection may rear; to smooth the path and turf the plats that surround the walks; to plant roses and eglantines, the holly, the cypress, the yew, the laurel and the bay; to invite the cool shade to protect from summer's heat, and let in the sunshine to moderate the winter's cold; to interweave the sweet brier and the vine by the side of the murmuring brook; to keep off the rude hands that disturb, mutilate and destroy, and to the peaceful undisturbed retreat invite the robin and the mocking bird to warble their sweetest lays

" And pour their full heart
In profuse strains of unpremeditated art."

And when the mother and the sister, the widow and the orphan, and the love lorn maiden shall come to look for the lost one, they may feel that

" They are within the door
That shuts out loss and every hurtful thing."

And though they may be weeping sad tears and bitterly wailing that there was

7

> " Not a pillow for his head,
>   Not a hand to smooth his bed,
>   Not one tender parting said,
>   —— Slain in battle !"

May the hand of sympathy lead them to the spot where the sad relic is softly inurned, and may they know that when the ladies of Virginia have undertaken to guard it, that

> " Somebody is watching and waiting for him,
>   Yearning to hold him again to her heart;
> There he lies with the blue eye dim,
>   And smiling, child like, lips apart:
> Tenderly bury the fair young dead,
>   Pausing to drop on his grave a tear;
> Carve on the wooden slab at his head,
>   Somebody's darling lies buried here."

And you, my friends, are invoked to help in this holy work; and when you have done this, then remember that the widow and the orphan require your help, and must never be permitted to suffer for food, or raiment, or home, or *light* for the orphan mind.